POLYSTYRENE FOAM CRAFT

POLYSTYRENE FOAM CRAFT

L L Lawrence

Chilton Book Company
Radnor, Pennsylvania

First published 1974 in the United States of America
by Chilton Book Company, Radnor, Pennsylvania.

Library of Congress Cataloging in Publication Data

Lawrence, L L
  Polystyrene foam craft.
  (Chilton's creative crafts series)
  1. Plastics craft.   2. Polystyrene.   I. Title.
TT297.L33   745.57   73-22390
ISBN 0-8019-6117-3
ISBN 0-8019-6118-1 (pbk.)

This book has been set in Monophoto Apollo by
Oliver Burridge Filmsetting Ltd, Priestley Way, Crawley, Sussex, England

Preface

This book has been written in the hope that it will introduce to all those interested in creative work the exciting possibilities of expanded polystyrene. The material has many advantages, not the least of these being its low cost, which will commend it automatically to students and teachers as well as to those who just feel the need to create and have not a purse to match their enthusiasm.

Expanded polystyrene can be cut with a razor blade, pen knife, fret-saw, pad-saw or heated tools, worked with sandpapers to a smooth finish, textured for bolder effects or grained to produce the effect of wood.

Any kind of paint can be applied to its surface. Water or poster colours take excellently, maintaining their chroma, which is so often lost on other materials. Acrylic paints and emulsions (or latex paints) are equally effective. Once the surface is sealed, oil-based paints, which serve to harden the work, or metallic paints, which give a surprisingly heavy appearance to this lightweight material, may be used. Finished pieces may be decorated with string, beads, etc., or covered with fabrics or metallic foils.

Teachers will find that this clean, easily worked material will allow for results which will increase the confidence of pupils or young students in handling three-dimensional work. For the hobbyist, working with expanded polystyrene will supply the essential ingredients of any hobby: the experience of total involvement in a project, and the satisfaction gained from the execution of a piece of work to the best of one's ability. For the experienced artist the possibilities are endless.

It is hoped that the examples and methods shown in this book will stimulate the reader to experiment further and find the pleasure in working this material that I have found, whether the end product be for pleasure or profit.

Acknowledgments

This book owes much to the assistance and co-operation received from many helpful and kindly people at Cassio College, Watford. I am particularly indebted to Mr H A Elliot, FRGS (now retired) and his successor, Mr J D G Thompson, BA, Dip. Ed., AMBIM. The co-operation of my Head of Department, Mr P W Blackwell, was much appreciated as was the help given by Mr K Forrow. Mr J Blaney, BSc., ACIPA, Cert. Ed., checked and supplemented my technical information. Mr T W Masters, Dip. FE, photographed students' work. To them my sincere thanks.

I am especially grateful to those colleagues, other artists, students and organizations who generously permitted their work to be included in the book, and to Mr John Burgess of Effective Services, who designed and produced the hot wire cutter described here.

Manufacturers of raw materials and products mentioned have been most helpful. Particularly, my thanks are due to Mr G F Andrews, M Inst. M, of Warmcelite for his patience in answering my queries, to Mr F A Gordon of Wall Paper Stores Ltd and to Mr P M Charlesworth of Monsanto Chemicals Ltd.

I am also grateful to Miss P Robinson of Retail Display Service whose help throughout the preparation of this book has been invaluable.

It is difficult to comprehend how these pages could ever have come together without the constant help of my wife, Edith, who tried hard to teach me to work in an organized fashion, dealt with typing and a considerable quantity of correspondence and cleared up after my home-based carving sessions. She earns my grateful thanks. Thanks also to my daughter Christine for her help in sorting photographs and text and who, together with the Knight family, spent several riotous hours test-flying expanded polystyrene gliders.

The following photographers have helped to illustrate this book:

Gordon P Hearth, Figs. 3, 10, 12, 14, 21-2, 27, 29, 40-55, 57, 59-61, 65-8, 71-2, 74-80, 81, 84, 87, 89, 90, 92, 101-2, 105-6, 108

Harry A Batchelor, Figs. 1, 2, 4-9, 11, 13, 15-19, 23-4, 26, 28-9, 31-9, 56, 58, 62, 64, 73, 85-6, 88, 91, 95, 107, 111-2, 114-8

Ronald Southwell, Figs. 20, 82, 93-4

R W Bradshaw, ABDS, Figs. 25, 83

T W Masters, Dip. FE, Figs. 30, 109-10, 113

John Burgess, Fig. 100

Quo'tass (Photographers) Ltd, Figs. 103-4

James Butler, ARA, Figs. 121-2

Douglas C Morris & Co., Figs. 69-70

Contents

1 *What is expanded polystyrene?*

To answer this question properly it would be necessary to study the whole subject of plastics in depth. For our purpose it will be sufficient to describe briefly how expanded polystyrene actually comes into being.

First, a word about *polymers*. These are complex materials which are produced by polymerizing (joining up) the molecules of the original simple material to form larger molecules. In nearly all cases polymerization converts a liquid into a solid. Polystyrene is made by polymerizing the simple material, *styrene*, which is produced by combining benzene and ethylene. The polystyrene thus produced is one of the thermoplastic materials sometimes called *linear polymers*. These are materials which soften on the application of heat and harden as they cool. It is this property which allows polystyrene to be moulded into a variety of forms, such as sheets, blocks and rods, and to be expanded to produce the material with which the reader will be working.

In order to expand polystyrene, a material known as a *blowing agent* is introduced into it while it is in a molten condition. A blowing agent is a substance which is either readily converted into a gas (such as a low-boiling liquid like pentane) or a material which decomposes under the action of heat, giving off a gas (such as an azo compound, which gives off nitrogen).

The preparation of expanded polystyrene takes place in two stages. First, the blowing agent is introduced into the molten polymer, and secondly the material is extruded in the form of tiny beads. These beads are then subjected to heat, usually steam. The blowing agent within the beads is then converted into a gas, which causes expansion. The degree of expansion, may be seen by comparison of the beads before and after expansion (see Figs. 1 and 2). The expanded beads are then left, to allow the atmosphere to permeate them. They are then fed into moulds and more heat is applied. This heat fuses the beads

1

Fig. 1. The minute beads of polystyrene after extrusion. These beads now contain pentane and await expansion by the application of heat. (Courtesy Warmcelite Ltd)

Fig. 2. The beads after expansion. These are fed into moulds to be fused together. (Courtesy Warmcelite Ltd)

together and produces a further smaller expansion. The material taken from the moulds is expanded polystyrene. The density of the material will depend on the ratio of blowing agent to polystyrene or, more simply, how much the beads are expanded.

Several grades of density of expanded polystyrene are produced. The standard grade of the material is of 1 lb. density, that is, one cubic foot weighs 1 lb. For very fine sculpture work material of 2 lb. density will make working easier. In an attempt to 'play fair' all work in this book by the author is produced in the least expensive, standard grade material. A self-extinguishing grade is produced by the introduction of certain additives, such as sodium silicate. This grade is used as a structural material, usually for insulation and for display and exhibition work.

Expanded polystyrene is a chemically inert product and will therefore not rot. Having no food value it will neither attract or support moulds. The material does not flake or irritate the skin and so may be handled with complete safety.

However, the following points cannot be overstressed. The author must be forgiven for making reference to precautionary measures on more than one occasion in the text of this book.

1 The material is highly inflammable. When burning it gives off a fierce heat and produces a thick smoke. Even the self-extinguishing grade will drip hot

material if flame is applied to it. So keep the material clear of heat sources when working with it. If the reader has a large quantity, he should store it outside, where it will come to no harm if it is well wrapped in paper.

2 The other hazard comes when the material is being sanded or turned. This produces a fine dust which should not be inhaled, so always wear some kind of face mask for protection.

3 When the material is cut with heat, wisps of smoke will occasionally rise from the cutting tool. Most of this smoke is caused by residue on the tool burning inefficiently. Keeping tools clean will cut this smoking to a minimum. The smoke is composed of carbon dioxide with a trace of carbon monoxide. As far as the author can ascertain, the small amount of smoke produced by the craft worker does not constitute a health hazard. Nevertheless, for those cutting constantly over long periods for professional purposes, good ventilation or an extractor fan would seem to be a sensible precaution.

A fair summing up would be to say the material is clean, non-irritating and, when reasonable precautions are taken, quite safe.

2 *Requirements for working*

The minimum requirement for starting a piece of sculpture is a block of expanded polystyrene of a suitable size and a penknife, preferably one with a long, thin blade or one ground to a suitable shape. However, to exploit the material to the full, the following tools and materials will be found helpful, and for some work essential.

Paper and pencil for preliminary drawings of the proposed work
Thin card for cutting templates (card a little thicker than post card is ideal), scissors, pins, razor blade
A small carborundum ⓡ stone to keep sculpturing knives razor sharp
Fine sandpaper, emery paper
A small soldering iron, or other means of cutting by heat
Adhesive
Paint of your choice for applying finish

Other tools and materials required for working expanded polystyrene will be discussed in detail in later sections.

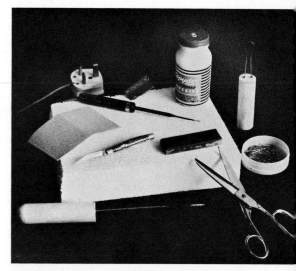

Fig. 3. It is encouraging to note that these low-cost tools and materials are the only ones required to produce almost all the work pictured in this book.

3 *Cutting expanded polystyrene*

One of the outstanding advantages of expanded polystyrene is the ease with which it may be cut. Carpentry tools are useful for the first rough cutting of large pieces of work, while a variety of knives and blades may be used for delicate carving. Where accuracy is of prime importance, cutting is best effected with heat. All these methods will now be considered separately and in some detail.

CARPENTRY TOOLS
The hand-saw

Straight cuts through material from 2 in. (5 cm.) to 1 ft. (30·5 cm.) thick are easily made with a hand-saw. This saw does not produce a perfectly clean cut so its use should be confined to the quick cutting of large blocks into workable sizes.

The pad-saw (or key-hole saw)

This saw produces a similar cut to a hand-saw but has the advantage of being able to cut shapes other than those composed of straight lines. This tool is recommended for cutting material from 2 in. (5 cm.) to 6 in. (15·2 cm.) thick.

The fret-saw

This saw produces a much finer cut and can cut fairly intricate shapes. The fret-saw works best on material from 2 in. (5 cm.) to 3 in. (7·6 cm.) thick.

RAZOR BLADES, PENKNIVES AND CRAFT KNIVES

It is essential that all blades used should be sharpened frequently on a carborundum ⓡ stone in order to maintain a good edge. Examination of a piece of expanded polystyrene will show that the material is a compression of small beads. Blunt blades will tend to pull these beads from the surface and leave unsightly holes.

Razor blades

The single-edged types are the only kind which are safe to use and will cut $\frac{1}{2}$-in. (1·3-cm.) material perfectly. Double-edged blades in metal holders do not expose enough blade to effect a good cut.

5

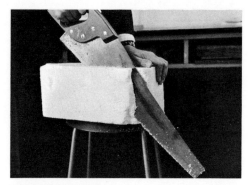

Fig. 4. The hand-saw.

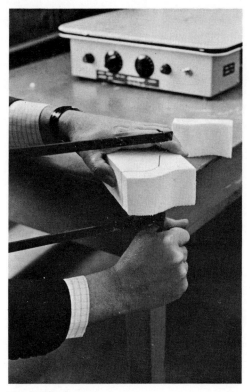

Fig. 5. The pad-saw.

Fig. 6. The fret-saw.

Craft knives and penknives

Many excellent craft knives are available and it must be left to the reader to choose a type which produces the best results for him. Probably the most effective cutting edge is a penknife with a long, thin blade, or one ground to a suitable shape. Such knives will cut $\frac{1}{2}$-in. (1·3-cm.) and 1-in. (2·5-cm.) material easily and efficiently. However, they are employed to best advantage when used for sculptural work. Before starting such work it will be found useful to explore the types of cut possible and to obtain the feel of the material.

Anyone with access to a grinding wheel may produce an excellent knife, tailor-made to suit the individual's particular requirements. Select a length of wood (thin dowel is ideal) to serve as a handle. With a tenon-saw cut a slot in the wood about 1 in. (2·5 cm.) deep. Take an old hack-saw blade and grind it to the required shape and length. Insert the blade into the slot and bind the handle with thin string to hold the blade firm. Then give the blade a keen edge by sharpening it on a carborundum ® stone. Much of the author's sculpture work pictured in this book was produced with such a home-made knife.

CUTTING WITH HEAT

The easiest and most efficient method of cutting expanded polystyrene is with heat, which may be applied in a variety of ways. We shall consider three methods: the hot needle cutter, the sol-

6

Fig. 7. A selection of knives. The three knives on the right were made by grinding down old hacksaw blades. The handle of the knife on the extreme right is leather-covered. The penknife in the centre has a blade which is ideal for carving. The craft knife on the left has a variety of interchangeable blades.

Fig. 8. Before starting sculpture work, experiment to see how many different-shaped cuts are possible. Holding the knife blade at varying angles will produce differing depths and widths of cut. Providing the knife is sharp, this cut in the side of the material will close up when the knife is withdrawn.

dering iron and the hot wire cutter. The efficiency of these methods is linked closely with their cost: the more efficient the method the more expensive the tool.

The hot needle cutter

A simple cutter may be made by fitting a steel knitting needle into a 4-in. (10·1-cm.) length of 1-in. (2·5-cm.) diameter dowel. The needle is then heated over a bunsen burner or ordinary domestic gas burner. Do not use this tool on the material while the needle is red hot.

It will be found that a needle tool placed in a gas burner for about 30 seconds will heat sufficiently to cut approximately 2 ft. (61 cm.) in length through $\frac{1}{2}$-in. (1·3-cm.) material. At this point the tool will have cooled to below the temperature at which it will cut effectively. It is therefore advisable to produce two such tools so that while one is being used the second is heating up.

The soldering iron

A small soldering iron of the type illus-

Fig. 9. Cutting with heat. A small soldering iron and the hot needle tool. Use emery cloth to keep the tools clean.

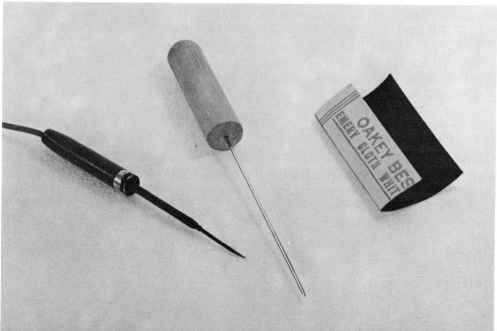

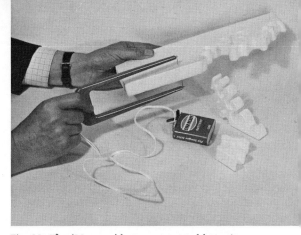

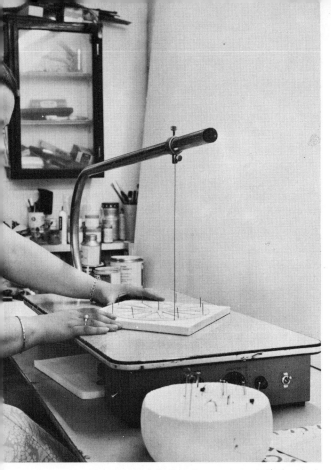

Fig. 10. An 'Almik' wire cutter in use. The work being cut is to form a part of the train panel pictured in Fig. 50. This is one example where accuracy and constant heat control of the hot wire cutter is essential.

trated in Fig. 9 is an efficient method of cutting the material, having the advantage of a constant heat supply. Care must be taken to hold both the needle cutter and the soldering iron vertically when preparing outer shapes for sculpturing.

Both the needle tool and soldering iron will build up a residue of the material after cutting. This residue may be cleaned off with emery paper.

The hot wire cutter

The reader will find that almost all the work illustrated in this book can be cut perfectly well with the hot needle tool or soldering iron. However, when the work needs to be cut with perfect accuracy, when the cut edges of the work need to be clean and crisp, then the hot wire cutter is the appliance to use.

The cutting is done by a thin wire, the temperature of which may be controlled to suit either the thickness of the material or the speed at which the cut is made. The angle of the wire may be altered to effect a bevelled cut and may be released to make it possible to cut out inner shapes.

The model pictured in Fig. 12 has a built-in sculpturing tool which is useful for producing large sculptural effects. This tool is also available as a separate unit.

The manufacturers of these cutters produce three models. The smallest has a table-top size of 16 in. × 10 in. (40·6 cm. × 25·4 cm.) and will cut material up to 6 in. (15·3 cm.) thick. The standard model has a table-top size of 28 in. × 15 in. (71 cm. × 38·1 cm.) and will cut material up to 12 in. (30·5 cm.) thick. The largest model has a table-top size of 39 in. × 20 in. (98·5 cm. × 50·8 cm.) and will cut material up to 14 in. (35·6 cm.) thick.

If used properly this machine will give long and efficient service. The author knows of one such machine which has operated for several hours each day over a period of five years without trouble of any kind. However, for best results the following rules should be observed:

1 Check with a set square that the wire is perfectly vertical—failure to do this will result in angled edges to the cut work;

2 Check that the wire is taut;

3 Select the heat which is right for the job being tackled—high heat for cutting large work quickly, low heat for cutting intricate shapes;

4 Never lift the machine by the bar supporting the wire;

5 Always switch the machine off when not in use. If this is not done the small amount of residue left on the wire after cutting will, because heat is still being applied to the wire, run down the wire and will after some time tend to clog the hole in the baseboard through which the wire passes. This in no way impairs the efficiency of the machine, but makes it difficult to replace the wire, should this become necessary;

6 Always cut over card templates. Do not run wood or metal along the wire because templates made of these materials cannot usually be made smooth enough to ensure good cutting.

These cutters are used extensively by those engaged in display and exhibition work. Many fine examples of work in expanded polystyrene executed with these cutters may be seen in shops and stores and at exhibitions.

Use of templates

Where accuracy is desired, all material cut by the heat methods discussed here

Fig. 12. Cutting round a template with a hot needle or soldering iron. It is important that the tool is held in the vertical position demonstrated. Note how the template is pinned to the material. Plenty of pins are used and are placed not too near the card edge.

should be cut round a template of thin card. Card somewhat thicker than postcard is ideal, because it is thin enough to cut easily with scissors or a craft knife, yet strong enough to take the heat of the cutting method employed. The card templates should be pinned securely to the material, near (but not too near) to the edges to be cut. Be sure that the pins are inserted vertically so that they do not foul the cutting needle, soldering iron or hot wire.

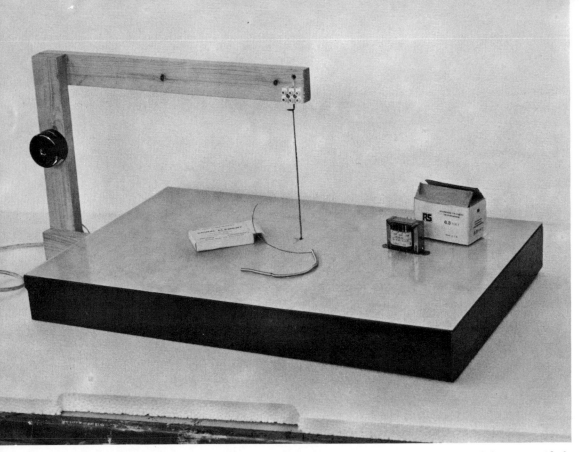

Fig. 13. The completed cutter. On the working top can be seen the transformer and spiral element specified. (Cutter produced by John Burgess)

MAKING A HOT WIRE CUTTER

It is reasonably simple to make one's own hot wire cutter, so these instructions have been included for those who feel they would like to try their hand.

Two requirements have to be met in order to produce a simple, single-heat hot wire cutter. First, it is required that electric current, passed through a transformer, must heat a thin wire to a suitable temperature. Too low a temperature will cut the material too slowly and make working tedious while too high a temperature will cut too fast to allow for accuracy and will 'burn back' under the template, reducing the size of the shape required and making it impossible to cut delicate forms. Secondly, the wire has to be supported so that it is kept taut. A slack wire will give under the pressure of the material being pushed on to it, which will result in cuts through the material which are not vertical.

The model considered in Fig. 13 has been designed with simplicity of construction and low cost, readily obtained materials and electrical components in mind. The woodworking involved may be tackled by anyone with minimum experience. Those with any doubts as to their ability to wire up the machine are advised to have this done by an electrician. It is important to use the wire and transformer specified below and to ensure that the length of wire is exactly as shown: a shorter wire will over-heat, a longer wire will not heat sufficiently.

10

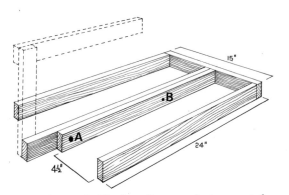

Diagram 1. The base frame ready to accept the baseboard and laminated plastic working top. Note the drilled hole at A through which triple-core wire and single-core wire passes and the drilled hole at B through which single-core wire passes when the machine is being wired up.

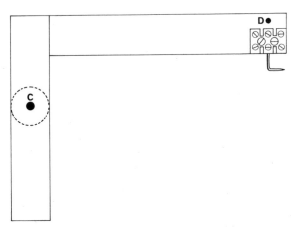

Diagram 2. The upright and supporting arm. The drilled hole at C is to accept the cable serving the switch. The hole at D is to accept single-core wire connecting the bent nail to the output of the transformer.

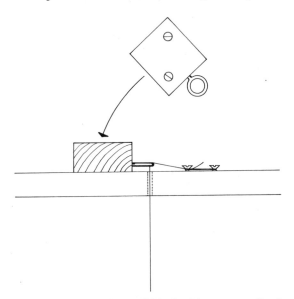

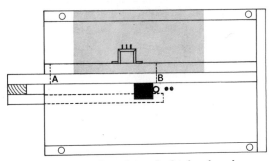

Diagram 4. View from beneath the baseboard. Dotted lines at A and B show drilled holes through which wiring will pass. The block holding the screw eye is shown in black. The shaded area indicates the position of the hardboard or peg-board shielding the transformer.

Diagram 3. The small block with screw eye fixed beneath the baseboard. Note the wire passing centrally through the hole in the baseboard, through the screw eye and twisted off round the two screw heads.

The materials required are as follows:

Lengths of 2-in. (5-cm.) and 1-in. (2·5-cm.) softwood: three lengths 23 in. (58·4 cm.), one length 27 in. (68·6 cm.), one length 17 in. (43·2 cm.), one length 15 in. (38·1 cm.), one length 12 in. (30·5 cm.).

A rectangle 24 in. × 15 in. (61 cm. × 38·1 cm.) of ¾-in. (1·9-cm.) chipboard or some similar stout material to serve as a baseboard

A similar-sized piece of laminated plastic to cover the baseboard

A 6·3 volt standard filament transformer

A 750 watt, 230/250 volt electric spiral element of the type used for bowl and bar fires

A terminal strip

A mains switch

Triple-core cable and single-core wire

Insulated staples

11

Impact adhesive, suitable screws, panel pins.

Refer to Diagrams 1–4 and proceed as follows:

Take three 23-in. (58·4-cm.) lengths of wood, one 27 in. (68·6 cm.) long and one 15 in. (38·1 cm.) long, and glue and nail them together as shown in Diagram 1. The central 27-in. (68·6-cm.) and 23-in. (58·4-cm.) lengths should be glued and screwed together. The dotted lines show positioning of the 12-in. (30·5-cm.) upright and the 17-in. (43·2-cm.) wire supporting bar to be fixed later. The 15 in. × 24 in. (61 cm. × 38·1 cm.) rectangle of chipboard should now be glued and screwed to the frame. Countersink the screws. Cover this baseboard with laminated plastic or a similar smooth-surfaced material, using an impact adhesive.

Take the 12-in. (30·5-cm.) and 17-in. (43·2-cm.) lengths of wood and screw together as shown in Diagram 2. Drill holes at C and D. The dotted circle shows the eventual positioning of the mains switch. Cut off three sections from the terminal strip and screw to the supporting arm as shown. Cut the head from a 1½-in. (3·8-cm.) nail, bend to a right angle and fix into the terminal strip.

Now place the upright in the position in which it is to be fixed and mark a point on the working top immediately below the hole in which the nail is held. This must be done accurately to ensure that the wire is absolutely vertical. Now drill a ⅛-in. (0·3-cm.) hole in the working surface at this point. Glue and screw the upright and arm to the frame.

An 18-in. (45·7-cm.) length of wire should now be taken from the spiral element. To do this, insert a knitting needle down the spiral and pull off the wire at right angles to the knitting needle. Make a small loop at one end of the wire and slip it over the bent nail. This allows for easy removal of the wire when cutting inner shapes. Thread the other end of the wire through the hole in the working top. Next it is necessary to ensure that the wire, when fixed, passes through the centre of this hole.

To effect this, cut a 2-in. (2·5-cm.) piece of 2 in. × 1 in. (2·5 cm. × 1·3 cm.) and screw a screw eye into it, as shown in Diagram 3. Do not screw into the end grain. Now screw this piece of wood beneath the baseboard so that the wire passes through the centre of the hole in the working top and through the screw eye. Apply a downward pressure to the supporting arm and twist the wire off round two screw heads placed as indicated in order to keep the wire taut. Screw the mains switch to the upright. The work so far needs no electrical expertise. It is worth emphasizing that the wiring is best done by a competent electrician. If all the woodworking is done and the components supplied, this will not be an expensive job.

Triple-core cable should now be led up the upright and taken through the hole marked C in Diagram 2 and through the mains switch. The triple core should now be led down the upright, under the baseboard, through the hole marked A and connected to the input of the transformer. The earth wire should be connected to the casing of the transformer.

Diagram 4 shows the positioning of the transformer. Two single-core wires are then taken from the transformer output. One wire is led through the hole marked B and wired to the screw eye while the other is led back under the baseboard, up the upright and along the wire supporting arm. This latter wire should be threaded through the hole marked D and fixed into the hole in the terminal strip which holds the bent nail.

Secure all wire neatly with insulated staples. The half of the base which houses the transformer should be shielded with hardboard or pegboard, as shown by the shaded area in Diagram 4. This will ensure that the transformer cannot be touched in any way.

Fix rubber stops to keep the machine clear of the table or bench on which it is placed. This will allow for a free passage of air around the transformer via the un-shielded areas at each end of the machine.

4 *Relief designs produced with heat*

This technique involves cutting a template of a proposed design and pinning it to the piece of material chosen to accept the work. The piece of material with the template attached is then held before an electric fire for a few seconds only, at a distance of about 6 in. (15·2 cm.). When the template is removed from the material it will be found that the card has protected the design area, leaving it in relief against the unprotected area which will have been etched back.

It must be remembered that expanded polystyrene is highly inflammable. Even the self-extinguishing grade, when burning, will drip hot material capable of inflicting painful burns. *It is therefore important that children should not use this technique unsupervised.*

Fig. 14. The relief effect obtained by pinning the card templates on the left over a rectangle of expanded polystyrene and exposing it to heat. The 'tile' on the right has not yet been painted or received any other finishing-off process. Such designs look very attractive on nursery ceilings or walls.

5 *Texturing*

The surface of the expanded polystyrene may be textured in one of three ways: manually, by heat or by corrosion.

MANUAL TEXTURING

This term is employed to describe the use of hand tools or the hand itself on the surface of the material. Cutting or scraping with files, knives, razor blades, saws, chisels etc., hammering with hammers of various sizes, or imprinting shapes into the surface under pressure, will all produce interesting, characteristic textures.

TEXTURING WITH HEAT

A simple wire texturing tool is easily made by bending a length of florist's wire round a thin dowel and fixing the ends into a 4-in. (10·2-cm.) length of 1-in. (2·5-cm.) diameter dowel. When heated this tool will create many effective incised patterns and textures. The looped wire may be bent to other shapes in order to create different effects. It is perhaps more convenient to produce a

Fig. 15. These four 5-in. (12·7-cm.) square 'tiles' are textured with hand tools and a razor blade. The top left texture is produced with hand-saw cuts; the bottom left tile has had a single-edged razor blade scraped across it; the top right texture is chisel-scraped; and the bottom right tile has been hammered.

15

number of wire tools each with a distinctive wire shape fashioned to create a particular effect, otherwise your one wire tool will have to be rebent each time the design needs to be changed.

A small soldering iron is useful for texturing. If the head of the iron is filed to a point, textures of great delicacy may be produced. The standard-size iron will produce large areas of bold textures.

Fig. 16. Tools for texturing with heat. A soldering iron, a sculpturing tool and a selection of easily made wire tools.

Fig. 17. Some of the textures which may be achieved with simple wire tools.

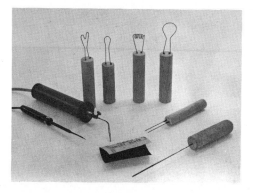

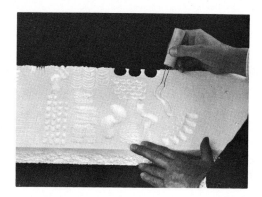

Fig. 18. R W Bradshaw, ABDS, demonstrating the application of textures with a heat tool of his own design. The power for the tool is supplied through a 3-volt transformer. Wire connectors from an old plug are fixed to a length of bakelite. These connectors serve to hold the heated wire. A micro switch operated with the forefinger allows for a certain amount of heat control.

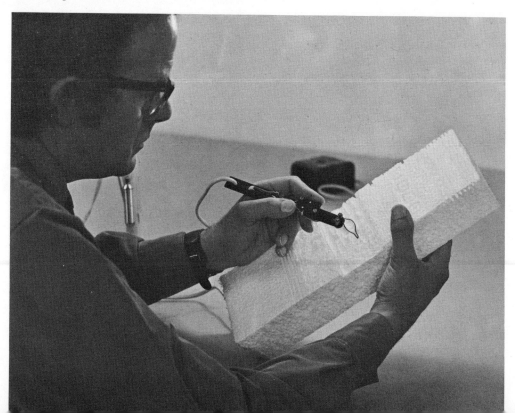

Fig. 19. This wall decoration (by R W Bradshaw), 18 in. (45·7 cm.) in diameter, has been textured with the tool pictured in Fig. 18.

Fig. 20. Bull Lyre (by Ralph Howell). This sculpture of an early Greek musical instrument is an excellent example of work textured with heat. The sculptor used hot knives, a soldering iron and a sculpting tool to produce the bold textures.

TEXTURING BY CORROSION

Many substances have a corrosive effect on expanded polystyrene. Although these effects are somewhat difficult to control, many interesting textures may be obtained by painting or spraying corrosive agents on to the material. Among these corrosive substances are carbon tetrachloride, cellulose paints, cellulose thinners, oil-based paints, metallic paints other than water-based, artist's fixative sprays, nail polishes and lacquers, and nail polish and lacquer remover.

Important. A face mask of the type sold by car accessory stores should always be used when spraying any of these substances.

It should be noted that carbon tetrachloride gives off harmful fumes and should never be used in other than a well-ventilated area.

Note also that cellulose paints and thinners are highly inflammable and should be used well away from heat sources.

The best safeguard is to read the instructions on any spray fixative, spray paint cans etc., and to take the precautions that the manufacturer recommends.

Fig. 21. The effect of carbon tetrachloride on expanded polystyrene.

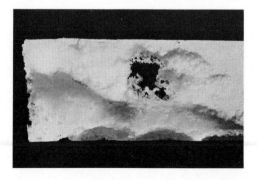

Fig. 22. 'Tiles' patterned by corrosion.

The piece of expanded polystyrene in Fig. 21 shows the effect when carbon tetrachloride is dripped on to the material. Very little control over the results of such experiments is possible, but some of the achievements might well be termed free form sculpture and be worthy of painting and glazing. This technique is useful for the creation of landscape features such as caverns, mountains and valleys for use with model railway layouts.

The 'tiles' in Fig. 22 show the effect of a corrosive gold paint on the material. The 'star' shape was merely painted with gold paint. The painted area then sinks below the surface and creates an intaglio design. The designs on the other three tiles are produced by painting the desired motifs with emulsion paint. When dry, the design is over-painted with a further application of emulsion paint. When the second coat is dry the whole tile is painted over with gold paint. The emulsion paint protects the design from the corrosive effect of the gold paint. The area of the tile without a design is 'etched' away, leaving the design in relief.

18

Fig. 23. This run of four panels symbolizing the seasons decorates a partition in a college refectory. The 5-in. (12·7-cm.) square tiles which form the panels are textured manually, by heat and by corrosion. They are coloured with emulsion paint and finished with a unifying glaze, produced by adding a little suitable emulsion paint to acrylic medium thinned with water. This work was produced by first-year Display students.

6 *Relief designs produced by corrosion*

Relief designs may be produced by corrosion in the following way.

Cut a template of the required shape and pin it firmly to the expanded polystyrene. Spray the template and any surrounding material which also needs to be 'etched' away with cellulose thinners

Fig. 24. Spraying a corrosive fixative on to expanded polystyrene over which is pinned a card stencil.

or a fixative of the kind used to fix charcoal or pencil drawings. An old bulb-type perfume spray would be ideal for spraying cellulose thinners; the fixative comes in convenient spray cans.

Cellulose spray cans, of the type used for re-touching car body work, will add colour to the 'etched' areas.

This corrosion technique has much the same effect as heat, but it does allow for more control over the design.

Fig. 25. After spraying and removal of the stencil. The top panel was produced without a frame.

7 *Applied textures*

We have so far been concerned with textures produced by scraping and cutting, by the application of heat and by spraying or painting corrosive substances on to the surface of the material. All these methods produce textures formed beneath the surface of the material. We will now consider those textures which may be applied to the surface.

GLITTER POWDERS

These powders, usually either grains of glass or tiny pieces of metallized plastic, are available in many colours including gold and silver, and in several grain sizes. Some glitter powders tarnish badly, so be sure that the glitter you select is labelled 'non-tarnishable'. They are readily obtainable from most stationers, and can often be seen on display during the pre-Christmas period. Should any difficulty be experienced in obtaining these powders, organizations dealing with display raw materials will be able to supply your needs.

Glitter powders are best applied over a still wet coat of emulsion paint. Place the work to be glittered on a sheet of paper. Apply paint as swiftly as possible

Fig. 26. This stylized reindeer, mounted on a base 9 in. (22·9 cm.) long, is covered with silver glitter powder. (By the author)

20

WE WELCOME YOU as a Chilton Creative Crafts Book user. We would like you to answer a few questions for us. If you have criticism to offer, we'd like to hear that too.

Name of book this card was in _____

☐ Hardcover ☐ Paperback

Where did you buy this book? ☐ Bookstore ☐ Department store book department ☐ College bookstore ☐ Crafts store

Other type of store (describe) _____

Was it ☐ Purchased for personal use? ☐ Received as a gift?
☐ Recommended reading? ☐ To be used as a crafts course textbook?

What is your age group? ☐ Under 15 ☐ 15-24 ☐ 25-39 ☐ 40-54 ☐ Over 55

Did you find this book
☐ Very complete ☐ Easy to understand ☐ Well illustrated
☐ Descriptive enough ☐ Hard to understand ☐ Poorly illustrated
☐ Lacking in detail ☐ Good value for money ☐ Not informative
☐ Poor value for money

Other (good or bad, please describe) _____

Do you work in the craft this book covered? ☐ Yes ☐ No ☐ Would like to ☐ Will use the book for guidance
☐ Do not intend to work in this craft at all

Indicate other crafts you are now involved in _____

What other crafts books would you be interested in? _____

May we send you a copy of our newest Crafts Brochure? ☐ Yes ☐ No

Other comments you may care to make _____

Name _____

Address _____

City _____ State _____ Zip _____

Fig. 27. The duckling, 12 in. (30.5 cm.) high, is textured with flitter powder.

so that the glitter powder may be shaken on to the work before the paint loses its adhesive quality. Surplus powder collected on the paper may then be reclaimed.

The colour of the paint should be chosen to form an 'undercoat' for the glitter powder colour selected. For instance choose white paint as an undercoat for silver glitter powder, yellow paint for gold glitter, red for red glitter, etc. Glitter powders used to texture expanded polystyrene provide a good finish to Christmas table pieces, wall decorations, etc.

FLITTER POWDERS

Flitter powder is composed of tiny pieces of coloured cellophane and is usually obtainable in pastel colours. It should be applied in the same manner as glitter powders. This material is not easy to obtain. It is sometimes stocked by large stationers, but enquiries directed at display organizations will probably be more fruitful.

FLOCKING

Flocking, composed of minute particles of rayon, is available in many colours. It may either be applied over wet paint

Fig. 28. This cat, only 5 in. (12·7 cm.) high, has been covered in black flocking. A tea strainer is useful for applying flocking to small work. (By the author)

in the same way as glitter and flitter powders, or sprayed directly on to the work. Spraying is only worth while when a large surface area has to be covered. Flocking imparts a warm, furry texture to work and is ideal for finishing small carved animal figures.

FELT AND FABRICS

Cutting or carving suitable shapes in expanded polystyrene and covering them with felt or fabric will produce superb exotic birds, fish and animal forms.

Attractive wall panels may be produced by applying felt or fabric to geometric shapes of varying thicknesses of the material. The shapes should then be fixed to a background which may itself be felt-covered. An infinite variety of

21

Fig. 29. This panel, measuring 21 in. × 36 in. (53·4 cm. × 91·4 cm.), consists of varying thicknesses of expanded polystyrene of different shapes. The faces of these shapes have been covered with coloured felt. (By Pearl Robinson)

designs is possible. Experiment with coloured felts to produce harmonious or contrasting colour effects. Contrast geometric shapes with abstract shapes and angular shapes with circles.

It will be found that a crisp edge to the felt is more easily achieved if the felt is glued to the cut shapes slightly oversize. When the adhesive is perfectly dry it can then be trimmed with sharp scissors or a knife.

The adhesive should be applied carefully, evenly and sparingly, otherwise it may seep through to the right side of the fabric or felt, appearing as an unsightly mark.

PLASTER

The application of plaster to the surface of finished work serves a dual purpose. Firstly, it provides a means of creating a variety of textures. For instance, a very different texture will be achieved by applying the plaster boldly with the fingers than will be obtained by stip-

pling the freshly applied plaster with an old toothbrush. Secondly, it will serve

Fig. 30. Peasant woman. This small figure, 9 in. (22·7 cm.) high, has been textured with a surface layer of plaster. (By Jill Sims, student)

22

Fig. 31. The Entertainer. The surface texture is produced by an application of textured paint over a coat of emulsion. The figure is 10 in. (25·4 cm.) high and is mounted on a block of 2-in. (5-cm.) material. (By the author)

to strengthen the work. It is quite surprising how rigid even a delicate piece of work will become after a surface application of plaster.

The plasters obtainable from home decorating stores for repairing cracks in walls and ceilings are ideal for texturing, because they have drying time which allows for work to be carried out on the surface. Plaster of Paris, having fast-drying properties, is not recommended for this purpose.

TEXTURED PAINTS

This technique imparts a heavy, stone-like quality to work. Sand-textured paints add greatly to the surface strength of the material. Excellent textured emulsion paints are available from most paint suppliers, but can be made at home by mixing silver sand, sawdust or ordinary builders' sand with emulsion paint.

The proportion of texturing material used will depend on what texture is required, but more than one-third texturing material to two-thirds paint may make the mixture difficult to apply. It is advisable to undercoat the work with emulsion paint before applying the textured coat.

STRING

The application of string allows for the addition of decorative effects which often cannot be produced in the material itself.

The area of the work to be covered with string texture or decoration should be lightly coated with adhesive and allowed to become perfectly dry. Lengths of string of the desired thickness should then be stretched between two convenient points and coated evenly with adhesive. This is best achieved by taking up a little adhesive between thumb and forefinger and running them along the string. Allow the string to dry thoroughly, and then cut it up into workable

Fig. 32. Some of the many ways in which string can be used to create decorative effects.

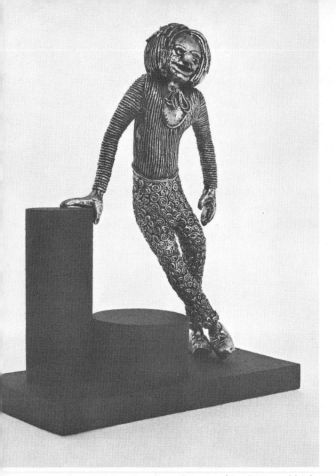

and shaping the foil carefully and applying it to the sculpture so that it fits snugly to the contours of the work. Metallic foils are available in rolls from some stationers or from suppliers of display raw materials. Several colours are produced, including gold and silver. Avoid the metallized plastic foils, as these will not retain their shape when curved.

PAPER-BACKED FOILS

Covering sculptural work with paper-backed metallic foil achieves a metallic effect which far surpasses the effects obtained with metallic paints.

Work with these foils requires considerable patience, and involves sticking small pieces of foil over the contours of the work. In order that the foil lays flat when overlaid, its edges should be 'feathered'. To do this, hold the foil

Fig. 33. This clown figure, 12½ in. (31·8 cm.) high, is textured with string. The figure is finished by lightly brushing gold paint over a dry coat of black emulsion. (By the author)

lengths. Do not allow these pieces of string to touch each other or they will stick together on impact and be very difficult to separate. The string may then be fed carefully on to the area to be decorated.

Experiment on a scrap of expanded polystyrene with string of differing thicknesses to discover how many varied textures and decorative effects may be produced.

METALLIC FOILS

Beautiful effects may be obtained by applying metallic foils to the surface of sculptured work. This involves cutting

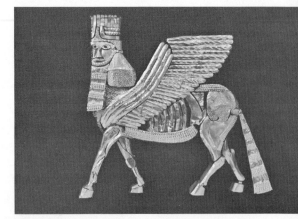

Fig. 34. This mythical beast is sculpted as a piece of low relief from 2-in. (5-cm.) material, then overlaid with gold metallic foil, carefully cut to fit the contours of the work. The panel, 2 ft 3 in. (68·6 cm.) long, is covered in hessian. The texture is achieved by indenting the foil over odd scraps of expanded polystyrene. These indentations are made either on the face or the back of the foil, according to whether a relief or intaglio design is desired. (By Dilys Hasted, student)

24

Fig. 35. Funeral mask. This work, taken from the Tutankhamen funeral mask, is covered with gold and blue paper-backed foil. (By Peter Curran, FRSA)

(metallic side uppermost) in the left hand and feather the edge by tearing downward and towards the centres of the pieces with the right hand. When the pieces are turned over it will be seen that the paper backing will have torn away from the edges. The edges of the pieces are therefore tissue-thin foil which makes it possible to overlay without any noticeable joins.

ACHIEVING A SMOOTH TEXTURE

A fine or flour-grade sandpaper, carefully used, will give a beautiful marble-like surface to expanded polystyrene. It is only possible to obtain perfectly smooth areas over large curved surfaces or over smaller areas not broken by detailed carving. Experience with the use of sandpaper will allow one to feel a 'grain' in the material and by sanding 'with the grain' damage to the surface can be avoided. Sanding will produce a very fine dust which will float in the air

and take some while to settle. Always use a face mask to guard against breathing in this dust. Even a handkerchief or scarf covering the mouth and nose will be preferable to ignoring this precaution. If the sanded work still shows imperfections, apply wet plaster and when this plaster is completely dry, sand to produce a perfectly smooth finish.

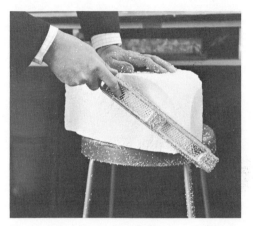

Fig. 36. When large, curved shapes are to be produced from blocks of the material, a file of the type pictured is useful to rough away material prior to final smoothing.

Fig. 37. Parrot. This work, 18 in. (45·8 cm.) high, is finished in gold metallic paint. The smooth surface is produced by applying plaster and sanding. (By Susan Pearmain, student)

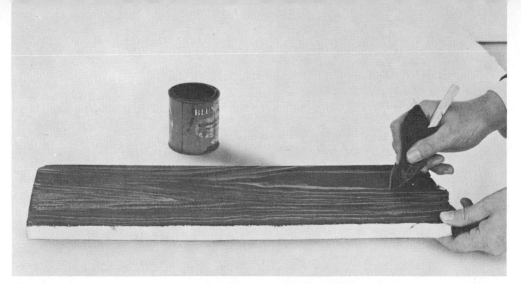

Fig. 38. Applying a wood grain to a length of 1-in. (2·5-cm.) material. Graining the material in this way produces realistic imitation oak beams which are easily fixed to walls with latex adhesive. Use the self-extinguishing grade for this work and keep the 'beams' away from heat sources.

Fig. 39. Another decor use for expanded polystyrene. Here ½-in. (1·3-cm.) material is cut to brick shapes, applied to the walls and finished with emulsion paint. Always use self-extinguishing grade for such interior work. (Courtesy K Forrow, MIGD)

WOOD-GRAINING

To effect a wood grain on expanded polystyrene proceed as follows. First, give the work a smooth finish with flour-grade sandpaper. If the work lacks such a finish, brush a fairly stiff application of plaster over its surface. Allow the plaster to dry, and finish by sanding. Then apply two good coats of cream emulsion paint to the work and allow that to dry. The emulsion paint should then be painted with a scumbling stain, which should be worked on immediately. This is best done by covering the handle end of an old toothbrush, or any similar smooth, round-ended object, with a soft cloth and wiping away the stain to produce the desired grain. Blur the grain produced by lightly laying a dry brush over the work. If a gloss finish is desired, apply varnish when the stain is thoroughly dry.

8 *Sticking expanded polystyrene*

Like some paints, many adhesives have a corrosive effect on expanded polystyrene. It is therefore essential that the correct type of adhesive is selected. There are several adhesives designed for expanded polystyrene, but these are primarily for fixing the material to other materials; for instance fixing ceiling tiles to ceilings. We, however, are concerned with the efficient fixing of expanded polystyrene to expanded polystyrene, and for this purpose the rubber-based adhesives are the only types safe to use. The cream-textured latex adhesive available from stationers is ideal. It is sold in tubes, small bottles and large tins. For best results the adhesive should be applied sparingly to both surfaces to be joined and allowed to dry. When quite dry (in normal room conditions after about ten minutes) the adhesive will feel rubbery to the touch.

The pieces to be joined should then be brought together. The bond will be made on impact and so it is important that this operation is carried out with great care. Should the pieces be brought together inaccurately it will be found very difficult to part them. Ruined work is often the result of an attempt to part material fixed by this impact method.

For some fixing where, for instance, interlocking is needed, the impact method is not suitable. In these cases the adhesive should be applied and the pieces joined together without delay. The only disadvantage of this method is that the adhesive will need several hours to dry and effect a good join.

Latex adhesive is used for all work illustrated in this book, unless otherwise stated.

9 *Painting finished work*

Fig. 40. The camel, 8 in. (20·3 cm.) high, taken from an early Chinese ceramic, has been finished in gold metallic paint. An antique effect has been produced with metallic paint and poster colour in the manner described. (By the author)

The paint used should of course be selected with the subject in mind. Water colours, poster colours, acrylic paints and emulsion paints are all suitable and present no problems. However, as has already been mentioned, some paints have a corrosive effect on expanded polystyrene. If it is desired to finish work with oil-based gloss paint or metallic paints it will be necessary to first seal the material with at least two good coats of emulsion paint. Cellulose is highly corrosive and cellulose paint should not be applied as a finish to expanded polystyrene.

Beautiful antique effects can be produced by finishing work with metallic paint, allowing it to dry and then coating the whole work with black poster colour, taking care to work the poster colour into all crevices. The whole work should then be wiped with a damp clean rag. The black will hold in the crevices imparting a realistic antique finish. The poster colour may then be held by an application of varnish.

28

10 *Pagoda, dome and spire shapes*

In order to produce these shapes it is essential to start with material which is a perfect square at the base. The template must be cut carefully and centred accurately on the block of material.

Diagram 5 indicates how the template (shaded area) is placed on the block and cut through on two sides. If a hot needle

Diagram 5.

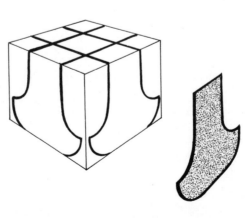

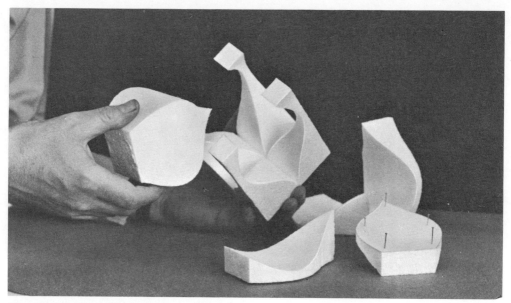

Fig. 41. A cut dome shape.

or soldering iron is used it is essential that the tool is held perfectly upright. A hot wire cutting machine will produce the best results.

It will be found that the discarded outer portions of the block have fascinating shapes. In fact these shapes mounted on a panel make interesting three-dimensional design features.

Also illustrated in Diagram 5 (on the left) are three of the many possible template shapes (shaded areas). The lower template will achieve an arch shape when the inner area is discarded.

Fig. 42. This 12-in. (30·5-cm.) pagoda is a good example of careful use of a hot wire cutter. It is finished in black, and decorated with small spots of gold. (By Pearl Robinson)

30

11 *Bending expanded polystyrene*

The ease with which the material can be bent to a curve will depend on its thickness and length. Very thin sheets bend quite easily, but if it cannot be bent to the desired shape without placing undue stress on it, expanded polystyrene $\frac{1}{2}$ in. to 1 in. (1·3 cm. to 2·5 cm.) thick can be curved in the following way.

First make parallel 'V'-shaped cuts in the material. Paint adhesive into these cuts and when the adhesive is dry, bend the material into a curve. The 'V'-shaped cuts will close and adhere on impact. If the work is large, it is advisable to cut a shape of material to back up the curve and hold it. (See Diagram 6.)

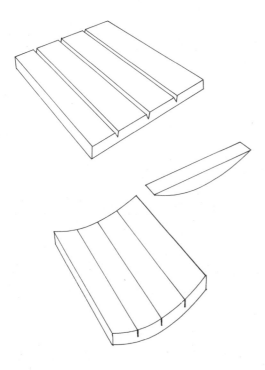

Diagram 6.

12 *Shaping by turning*

By taking an electric drill with a sanding plate attachment and sticking a block of expanded polystyrene to the plate, and by using fine sandpaper as a tool, many beautiful shapes may be turned.

The block of material should first be shaped roughly by using the method applied when making the pagoda shapes. This is advisable because in the early stages of sanding one is enveloped in a 'snowstorm' of the material, and the less material that has to be 'turned off' the better.

Sanding tools may be made by gluing sandpaper to curved shapes of expanded polystyrene; or the sandpaper may be held in the hand.

When gluing the block of material to the sanding plate, apply adhesive liberally to both surfaces. Allow to dry thoroughly, then centre the block carefully on the plate and press on firmly.

Cover the nose and mouth with a mask for protection against the fine dust produced when the material is being turned.

Material which stands more than about 8 in. (20·3 cm.) off the sanding plate will tend to spin off, and so, if using a drill with a small sanding plate, it is advisable to keep turning work within this measurement.

Fig. 43. Producing a dome shape by turning.

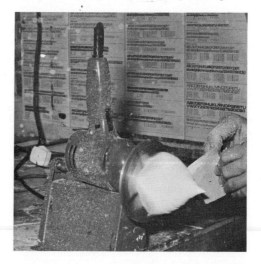

32

13 *Expanded polystyrene as a mould*

Expanded polystyrene makes an excellent and simple mould for plaster casting. Cut the shape of the proposed casting in the material and glue the outer shape securely to a piece of heavy card or hardboard. Coat the inside of the mould with soft soap or petroleum jelly, which will later assist the release of the plaster from the mould. Fig. 44 shows the mould ready to accept the liquid plaster.

Plaster of Paris is recommended for casting: it is inexpensive and quick-setting. Because plaster of Paris dries by chemical action, it is important that it is mixed correctly. Add the plaster to the water to achieve the mix, and add the correct amount the first time. Any plaster mixed in later will not be subject to the chemical drying process for the same length of time as the original plaster. This will produce a weak casting.

After pouring the plaster, tap the mould sharply to release any trapped air bubbles. The plaster will generate heat while it is drying and will be ready

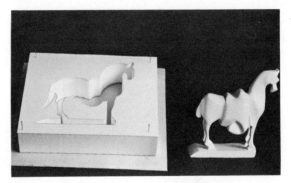

Fig. 44. Plaster carving by Margaret Stewart, student.

for removal from the mould when cold to the touch.

It is usually necessary to break the expanded polystyrene mould away from the plaster. This operation should be carried out with care to avoid breaking any delicate portions of the plaster casting. The plaster shape may now be carved with a sharp tool of one's choice.

The completed plaster animal shown on the right of Fig. 44 was produced from the mould on the left.

14 *Fixing to exterior walls*

Because of the spongy nature of the material, it is not possible to fix it to a wall with rawlplugs in the normal way. Efficient fixing may be achieved by cutting lengths of aluminium tube which are slightly shorter than the depth of material through which the tube is to be passed. The diameter of the tube should be selected so that the screws chosen fit the tube snugly.

Using a hot needle tool or soldering iron, bore holes in the material slightly smaller than the tubes. These tubes, coated on the outside with PVA glue, should then be pushed home flush with the back of the work. Hold the work up to the wall and mark through the tubes points where rawlplugs may be placed.

Then push the screw through the tubing and screw into the rawlplug until the screw head and washer come firmly up against the tubing. The screw head and washer will now be sunk just below the level of the material, and the depression may be made good with either plaster or a piece of expanded poly-styrene cut to fill the hole. (See Diagram 7.)

Diagram 7.

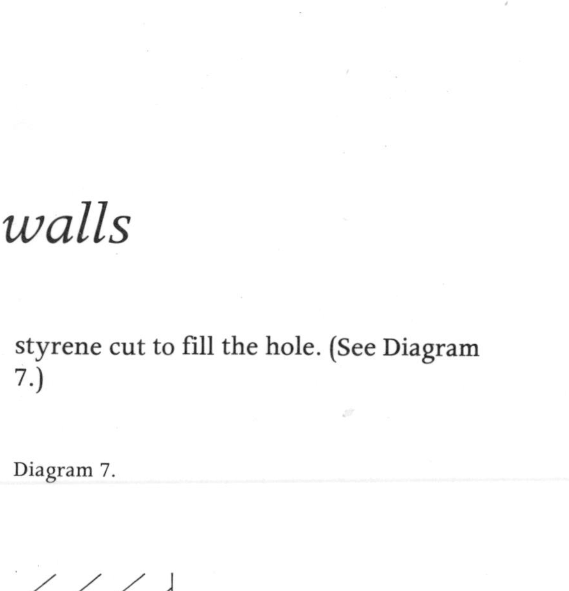

Fig. 45. This faithful reproduction of a fragment of the Parthenon frieze is fixed to an exterior wall in the manner described. Note how well the effect of broken marble is reproduced. The work is about 5 ft (52·4 cm.) long. (By Annette Smee, student)

15 *Strengthening, repairing, cleaning and mounting*

The versatility of expanded polystyrene has by now, I hope, been thoroughly demonstrated. One virtue, however, which the material does not possess is the ability to take a really hard knock. In compression the material is quite strong (a foot square cube of expanded polystyrene will easily bear the weight of an average man), but long and narrow forms tend to snap under tension. The secret of success in working expanded polystyrene is to recognize its weakness in certain forms and to choose subjects which avoid them.

STRENGTHENING WORK

The surface of expanded polystyrene may be strengthened by painting the work with textured emulsion, acrylic or oil-based paint and by applying plaster, glitter powder or string. Delicate portions of small carvings, i.e. the legs of small carved figures, may be strengthened by inserting plastic or wooden cocktail sticks. If matchsticks or small lengths of wood are used, be sure to sharpen the end to be pushed into the material, as a blunt end will be difficult to insert. For strengthening larger work, thin metal rods or dowel sticks may be used.

The most effective way to strengthen expanded polystyrene work is to overlay the surface with polyester filler paste. This is the product more usually employed to repair dents and holes in automobile bodies. The filler is supplied in two parts, paste and hardener, which are mixed together to form a paste which sets rock hard. The paste, once mixed with the hardener, sets quickly, so only small quantities should be mixed at one time.

Carvings to be covered with polyester filler paste should be produced slightly smaller than required and the paste laid on with a palette knife or similar tool to bring the work up to the desired size. Once hard, the overlay of filler paste may be sanded, filed or worked to a texture with a sharp, pointed tool. Manufacturers' instructions on the use of polyester filler paste should be strictly adhered to. Particularly, the hardener should not be allowed to come into contact with the skin or eyes. It is advisable to mix the paste out of doors or in a well-ventilated room.

Note. Do not underestimate the strength of the material. It should be mentioned that no work by the author pictured in this book has needed strengthening structurally.

REPAIR WORK

Most damage to small work displayed in the home will come about from pieces of carved work being knocked from tables, shelves etc., resulting in thin portions of the carving snapping off. Luckily these breaks are easily repaired.

Because expanded polystyrene tends to break around the bead-like structure of the material, a natural interlocking break occurs which assists the correct replacing of the pieces. If legs or arms of figures are snapped off it is helpful to insert, before gluing, a thin piece of wood sharpened at both ends into the pieces to be joined. If this extra strength is not necessary, just place adhesive on each piece to be joined. Bring the pieces together carefully, feeling for the interlocking which will ensure that the material joins in the correct position. If any adhesive is forced to the outside of the join it should be wiped away at once with a damp rag. The work should then be put on one side until the adhesive is set. Normally no retouching is necessary, but should paint be chipped off around the break, this can easily be made good.

The lightweight nature of the material, which allows for easy fixing of large wall panels and which makes it so easy to work, can also be a disadvantage.

Visitors to readers' homes may be astonished to see a 'heavy bronze' sculpture being blown off a sideboard by a breeze from an open window. The reader will only be annoyed! Damage of this sort is easily avoided by mounting work on wooden bases, by hollowing base areas and filling the hollow area with plaster, or by inserting nails into the base. All these methods serve to increase the weight of the work.

DAMAGE TO EXTERIOR WORK

Sun and rain have no effect on expanded polystyrene, although extremely heavy hail could mark the surface and severe frost will cause pitting. Perhaps the worst hazard is that some of our less discerning feathered friends occasionally peck it. It is to be hoped that they do not eat it, for it has no food value and must be very indigestible. It may be that the birds have recognized the high insulating qualities of expanded polystyrene and see it as good nest-lining material! The answer is to paint work designed to be sited outdoors. The author has no knowledge of exterior work being damaged by birds when this is done. Paint will also afford some protection against hail and complete protection against frost.

CLEANING

Unpainted work attracts dust and soon discolours. To restore the whiteness of the material, just put the work into a bowl or bath of warm soapy water. Do not push delicate work under the water. The buoyancy of the material is so great that this may snap off delicate portions. If the work is painted with emulsion paint, oil-based metallic paint or oil paint, clean in the same manner. Water will not affect any parts of the work adhered with latex adhesive.

MOUNTING RELIEF WORK ON PANELS

Panels may be of expanded polystyrene either textured or painted or both. Wall board, of which many types are available, is probably the best material for this purpose. This board is strong enough to have fabric, felt or hessian stretched round it without bowing. Before gluing on the relief work insert a loop of wire through the covered background to serve as a hook for hanging. When the work is glued to the panel it will cover the wire.

Fig. 46. A 2-ft. diameter circle mounted on a panel of expanded polystyrene. It has three coats of emulsion and is finished with bronze aerosol paint. (By Judith Mollison, student)

16 *Simple cut-outs*

This method of producing design work in expanded polystyrene merely involves applying shapes in silhouette to a background. No sculpturing is required, because any rounded effects can be produced with paint. Prepared animal shapes provide interesting painting exercises for young children. In the home, pleasing bathroom panels may be produced as simple cut-outs.

Fig. 47. A bathroom panel, 4 ft (21·9 cm.) long, finished in pale green emulsion paint and highlighted with white. (By the author)

17 Three-dimensional work—the 'layer' method

Before commencing three-dimensional work using the traditional methods of sculpture it will be useful to consider a method which we shall term 'layering', where a three-dimensional effect is produced by building up the work in layers of the material. These layers may be either of the same or varying thickness.

Follow these main steps:

1 Make a drawing of the subject on thin card. This drawing should indicate the height to which each area is to be raised;

2 Cut out the whole design to produce a template, and use this to produce a shape from the material. This shape serves as a background on which to build up the work;

3 Cut out that area of the whole card template which is to form the first layer. This produces a second template from which further shapes of the material are cut;

4 Stick the first layer to the background shape.

If the work calls for further layers, reduce the second template to produce a third one and so on until the final layer is applied.

If the square edges of the layers are rounded with a knife or sandpaper,

Fig. 48. This clown figure, 3 ft 6 in. (106·6 cm.) high, is a simple example of 'layered' work. Painted with emulsion paint. (By the author)

more realism is achieved. This should be done before the layers are glued into position.

This method is ideal for relief work which is to be mounted on a panel, and for beginners it will be a good introduction to the more demanding requirements of traditional methods of sculpture.

Fig. 49. The cockerel, 3 ft (91·4 cm.) high, has a small amount of sculpted work added. Painted with emulsion paint. (By the author)

Fig. 50. Here the author is shown building up a more intricate piece of 'layering'. Templates used in the build-up of this work may be seen on the bench.

Fig. 51. Incised sculpture. A knife produced the outline and a soldering iron the mane texture here. (By the author)

18 *On sculpture*

There are many excellent books dealing in depth with sculpture, but it is not out of place here to mention briefly the traditional sculpture techniques. These techniques may be listed as follows:

INCISED SCULPTURE

This is little more than drawing with an incising tool, the varying depths of cut giving character to the work. Incised sculpture is easily achieved in expanded polystyrene using a knife, hot needle or soldering iron.

SUNK RELIEF

If the linear incisions of incised sculpture are rounded down from the background and up again into the body of the subject, the resulting intaglio work will approximate the sculpture method referred to as sunk relief, examples of which may be seen in the sculpture of Ancient Egypt. This is more elaborate and allows for more realism than incised sculpture although it has less impact than work executed in low relief.

Fig. 52. Sunk relief. This work was produced entirely with a knife. (By the author)

Fig. 53. Low relief. The lion was cut from 1-in. (2·5-cm.) material and shaped with a knife. The work was then sanded and applied to a background of 1-in. (2·5-cm.) expanded polystyrene. (By the author)

42

INTAGLIO RELIEF

True intaglio sculpture is carved as a hollow relief, producing a negative image. When such work has a plastic material pressed into it, a positive image is produced, i.e. hot wax pressed into a hollow mould produces a seal. It must be said that the production of hollow relief work in expanded polystyrene, although not impossible, would present many problems. However, a hollow mould could be easily produced by carving a positive image in the material, surrounding the work with a 'fence' and filling the area with plaster of Paris. When the plaster has set, the expanded polystyrene can be picked from the mould and the hollow relief will be left in plaster.

LOW RELIEF

Low relief or bas-relief means shaping the surface of the subject with the background cut away, the work standing only a small distance from the background surface. One only has to consider the low-relief work on a coin to appreciate how light and shade acts on the very smallest depth of sculpture. Low-relief work in expanded polystyrene is best carried out by cutting the design and applying it to the background after sculpturing.

HIGH RELIEF

In high relief the features of the work stand higher than work produced in low relief, and the work may even be undercut to such an extent that only small areas of the sculpture remain as part of the background. Such work, although almost fully sculptured, is still intended to be viewed from the front. It may be executed in expanded polystyrene in the same way as low relief, except that thicker material should be used.

Fig. 54. High relief. The frog, mounted on a 13 in. × 13 in. (33 cm. × 33 cm.), hessian-covered panel, is finished in natural colour, painted with acrylic paint and glazed with an application of acrylic medium. (By the author)

SCULPTURE IN THE ROUND

This is sculpture executed without a background. It is therefore self-supporting and can be viewed from any angle. Sculpture in the round is possibly the most exciting way of exploiting to the full the advantages of working in expanded polystyrene.

Fig. 55. Sculpture in the round. This horse, taken from an early Chinese porcelain, is finished in dark green acrylic paint which has had a little acrylic medium added to produce a light glaze. The work is 8 in. (20·3 cm.) high. (By the author)

43

The sculptor in stone would consider his work ruined if he chipped an ear off a bust. The sculptor in expanded polystyrene may repair such an error, although obviously it is more satisfying to sculpt without repairs or additions. It is these 'short cuts' which may incur the scorn of the artist in stone or marble, but just as one exploits the advantages of charcoal, crayons, pastels, acrylic paints, mechanical tints, clay, plastics, etc., so one may justifiably exploit the advantages offered by expanded polystyrene.

Using this easily worked material should give the reader a feeling for sculpture which may lead him to experiment with more traditional materials.

Readers wanting a starting point from which to study traditional methods of sculpture would do well to refer to the sculpture of that most famous of all works of architecture, the Parthenon.

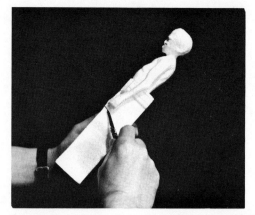

Fig. 57. The carving at half-way stage. The outline shape can be seen, as yet uncarved, on the lower half of the figure.

Fig. 58. The completed carving, finished in brown emulsion. The drum was added to increase interest. (By the author)

Fig. 56. The outline of the figure. Cut from 2-in. (5-cm.) material with a hot wire cutter over a template.

44

19 *Projects*

The following projects are arranged in order of degree of difficulty and deal with problems likely to be encountered by readers new to working with expanded polystyrene. Not all the projects will be of equal interest to all readers, but an attempt has been made to include a wide cross-section of work, so everyone will find something to suit his taste.

For the more experienced the projects will provide stimulation for more complicated or sophisticated work.

PRINTING WITH BLOCKS

This section is directed mainly at teachers and parents of young children. A small amount of time spent producing simple blocks will provide hours of pleasure for young children at home, or could form a basis for larger project work in schools.

First cut a suitable number of 4-in. (10·2-cm.) squares of hardboard, or similar rigid material, on which to mount the designs to be printed. Round off the sharp edges.

Now design simple shapes within 4-in. (10·2-cm.) squares and produce these in either ceiling tile or ½-in. (1·3-cm.) material. Use either a sharp knife or cut by heat round a template. These shapes may be incised with a knife, needle tool or soldering iron to produce inner patterns. The shapes should then be glued to the squares of hardboard. Shapes cut from 1-in. (2·5-cm.) or 2-in. (5-cm.) material will not need the hardboard backing.

Alphabet blocks may be made by cutting the shapes shown and incising the characters (in reverse of course) on the bases. Such blocks can be handled quite easily by young children.

Roll poster or emulsion paint on to a piece of hardboard to provide an even layer of paint. Press the blocks on to the rolled paint and transfer to the paper

Fig. 59. A group of primary school five-year olds enjoying a block-printing session.

Fig. 60. Inking up a block.

Fig. 61. A selection of blocks used in the printing session.

upon which the design is to be printed. Alternatively, apply the paint to the block directly from the roller. Suitable small rollers are obtainable from most hobby shops or artist's suppliers.

Light pressure of the block to the printing surface will reproduce the surface texture of the material with interesting results. Heavy pressure will produce solid colour.

Underwater scenes, Noah's Ark processions, playground activities, zoo visits, seaside scenes, etc., are subjects requiring only simple shapes to produce rewarding results.

A GLIDER

Much pleasure may be derived from the design and construction of model gliders from expanded polystyrene. Almost any 'glider-like' design will fly. The addition of weights such as nails or screws pushed into the nose will correct any tendency the glider may have to stall. It is surprising how many hard knocks such gliders will take. The only strengthening required is a strip of thin card stuck over the nose; this is a safeguard against a landing on a gravel path or similar rough ground.

The model pictured in Fig. 62 is constructed from a 2-ft. (60·1-cm.) square ceiling tile. Proceed as follows:

1   Take a 2-ft. (60·1-cm.) square of thin card. Divide it into 3-in. (7·6-cm.)

46

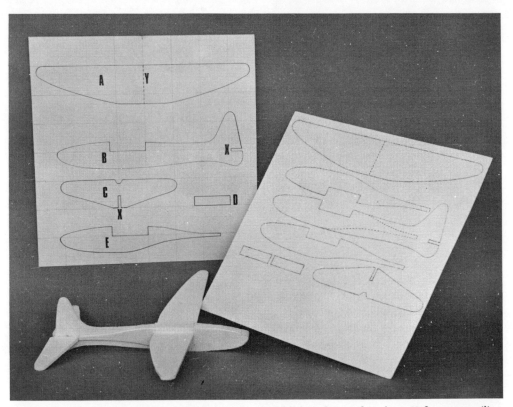

Fig. 62. The drawing was first planned on a piece of gridded card, transferred to a 2-ft. square ceiling tile (*right*), and then cut out and assembled.

squares and use the grid so formed to assist in the drawing of the glider shapes on the card.

2   Cut out the card shapes. Place them on the tile and using a felt-tip pen mark round the shapes. Shapes D and E should be marked twice.

3   Using a sharp knife, cut out the marked shapes. Take care to ensure that the slots in the tail plane and rear end of the fuselage, marked X, are fractionally narrower than the thickness of the tile. Ensure also that the cut-out to accept the wing is of a size that will ensure a snug fit.

4   Adhere shapes marked E to either side of the fuselage. Apply adhesive to tail plane cut-out and slot into fuselage so that the leading edge of the tail plane pushes up against the rear end of shapes marked E. Allow adhesive to dry.

5   Score with a sharp knife along the mid-way line of the wing shape marked Y. Cut about half-way through the thickness of the wing. Gently bend the wing to open the cut. Place adhesive into this cut and insert two spent matches to hold the cut open. This will give an uplift to the wing. Leave the model to stand until the adhesive is dry.

6   Apply adhesive to the wing slot in the fuselage. Press in wing shape. Check that the wing is balanced evenly in the fusilage.

7   Apply adhesive to the two oblong shapes marked D and fit into the wing slot above the wing. Leave to dry.

8   Cut a 4-in. (10·2-cm.) length of thin card and stick it to the nose area.

The glider is now ready to fly. It may be found that a $\frac{1}{2}$-in. (1·3-cm.) screw placed centrally in the nose will improve flight performance.

47

ABSTRACT FLOWER HOLDERS

Normally when flowers die and have to be thrown out the empty vase is placed out of sight. Flower holders of the type illustrated in Fig. 63 make attractive, decorative shapes even without the flowers they are designed to hold.

Countless interesting abstract forms are possible. Let the pencil fly freely over the paper and then select the shapes that appeal. Harsher forms are achieved by using straight lines and angles in the designs.

To provide a water supply for the blooms, cut holes carefully in the holder. These holes should be of a size to accept 35-mm. film cassette containers or any other non-rusting container which may be suitable.

Fig. 63. Flower holder. (By Pearl Robinson)

MOBILE CONSTRUCTION

The construction of mobiles is a fascinating exercise in movement in three dimensions. Mobiles are increasingly finding a place in home decoration. Moving in the slightest draught, their changing shapes are a source of constant interest. The lightweight nature of expanded polystyrene makes it ideal for mobile construction. Suspension hooks (p. 59) are easily fixed to it and the insertion of a small nail or two where appropriate will correct in balance.

Mobiles derive their impact from the changing shapes, not only of the individual pieces, but of the design as a whole. It is therefore important that the design is not merely a suspended 'roundabout'. This undesirable effect can be avoided by ensuring that the single cotton suspending the whole design is placed off centre.

Expanded polystyrene ceiling tiles are excellent for the shapes, although the addition of shapes in thicker material make the mobile more interesting.

Cotton is ideal for suspending the whole mobile and the individual shapes. If the lengths of cotton between individual shapes are too short, free movement of the mobile will be inhibited.

48

Never use nylon thread on mobiles. Nylon is far too rigid to facilitate steady, easy movement through the air, which is so essential.

Diagram 8. A simple mobile construction, showing how the movement of the design will create constantly changing shapes. Note the holes cut in the material which not only add interest but assist the balance of the design. This mobile may easily be constructed from ceiling tiles. Simple shapes, to which photographs of pop stars, sportsmen, etc. are glued, make fine animated pinboards.

CASTING PLASTER TABLE LAMP BASES

1 First, decide on the size required for the completed plaster lamp. Then cut four rectangles of the material so that when they are glued together the inner dimensions will be those of the shape desired. A suggested inner size for the casting is $4\frac{1}{2}$ in. × $4\frac{1}{2}$ in. × 7 in. (11·4 cm. × 11·4 cm. × 17·8 cm.). Expanded polystyrene 1 in. (2·5 cm.) thick is ideal. Ceiling-tile material may be used if reinforced on the outside with heavy card. If the suggested inner size is chosen and 1-in. (2·5-cm.) material is selected, it will be necessary to cut two pieces of material $4\frac{1}{2}$ in. × 7 in. (11·4 cm. × 17·8 cm.) and two pieces $6\frac{1}{2}$ in. × 7 in. (16·5 cm. × 17·8 cm.).

2 Now decide what decoration to have on the completed plaster base. If the design is to be in relief, then it will be incised into the expanded polystyrene rectangles. For this a knife, hot needle, texturing tool or soldering iron may be used. If the design on the completed base is to be an intaglio one, then the designs will be added to the rectangles. These additions should be thin shapes of expanded polystyrene stuck in the

required positions on the rectangles. The finished work will gain in interest if these shapes are of varying thicknesses. Both these methods, of course, can be used together, i.e. some areas can be cut below the surface and others built up.

A severe relief design may be obtained in the following manner.

Take a rectangle in either $\frac{1}{2}$-in. (1·3-cm.) or ceiling-tile material. With a knife, cut the required design right through the material, discarding the cut-out shapes. An identical rectangular shape should then be glued to the back of the first rectangle.

If $\frac{1}{2}$-in. (1·3-cm.) or ceiling-tile material is used for backing up the first rectangle, then it is advisable to strengthen the rectangle with heavy card.

3   The design, produced by whichever method is chosen, is then made on the rectangles. These rectangles have to be glued together, so do not continue the design right up to the edges of the two wider shapes. It should not extend nearer than $\frac{1}{2}$ in. (1·3 cm.) from the top of the rectangles.

4   Now glue the four rectangles together (see Diagram 9). Coat the inside of the mould with petroleum jelly or soft soap, making sure that this reaches into all the crevices. This will facilitate easy removal of the expanded polystyrene from the finished casting.

5   Now cut a length of 2 in. × 1 in. (5 cm. × 2·5 cm.) soft wood which should be $\frac{1}{2}$ in. (1·3 cm.) shorter than the height of the mould. Glue to this wood a strip of expanded polystyrene which has a 'V'-shaped cut made in it to accept the flex.

6   A small notch should be cut in the wood to allow the flex to pass through the fitting illustrated, which should now

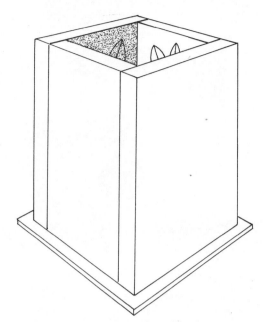

Diagram 9. The four rectangles of expanded polystyrene glued together. A leaf design is incised on the inner walls. The base is in position for gluing.

be screwed to the top of the wood. (It will only be possible to use two of the three screw holes provided in this fitting.)

7   Thread flex through the screw thread fitting and down the channel formed by the 'V'-shaped cut.

8   Cut a piece of hardboard or wood, a little larger than the base of the mould to serve as a baseboard. Screw the wood column holding the flex to the baseboard so that the screw thread fitting lies in the centre of the inner square.

9   Now cut a small notch in one side of the mould so that the flex might be led through it. Using PVA glue, fix the mould to the baseboard. Apply weight to the top of the mould and leave until glue has set.

10   With a brush apply petroleum jelly or soft soap to the baseboard inside the mould.

11   Press a little plasticine round the

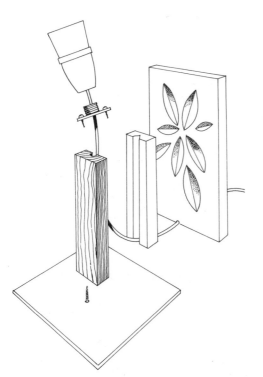

Diagram 10 (not to scale). The wood and expanded polystyrene columns, the latter with the 'V' cut to accept the flex. The small notch in the top of the wood will accept the flex when the screw-top fitting is screwed to the wood. These fittings usually have three holes to accept screws, but it will only be possible to use two of these, as the third will be over the expanded polystyrene. The hardboard base is shown with the screw protruding and ready to be screwed into the wood. Note the flex leading out through a small notch cut at the base of one side.

screw thread fitting to protect it from the plaster when it is poured. The notch through which the flex is led out should also be well plugged with plasticine.

12　Wrap string or adhesive tape round the outside of the mould to provide strength against the weight of the plaster. Check that there are no bad joins through which plaster might seep.

13　Mix plaster of Paris, as previously described on p. 33 and pour in until it

just covers the base plate of the fitting into which the lamp holder is screwed.

Tap the mould sharply to release air bubbles which may be trapped in the mould.

14　Allow plaster to set and carefully break away the expanded polystyrene. Unscrew the baseboard, remove plasticine seal from screw thread fitting and gently ease flex until it moves freely through the plaster. Wire up lamp holder and screw down on to fitting.

15　Seal the plaster with a clear lacquer and finish as desired.

16　Cut a square of felt and glue with PVA glue to the base.

For larger castings, choose thicker material or strengthen with hardboard. The weight of plaster within large moulds may be reduced by gluing strips of expanded polystyrene round the centre column, thus taking up space which would otherwise be filled with plaster.

Fig. 64.

A 'LAYERED' OWL

For this project use either $\frac{1}{2}$-in. (1·3-cm.) material or expanded polystyrene ceiling tiles.

Refer to Diagram 11 and the following instructions.

1   Cut template of whole owl and produce a shape in expanded polystyrene. Subsequent shapes will be added to this form.

2   Cut away and discard wings from template, produce the resulting shape in the material and place on first shape.

3   Cut away ears from template and discard. Cut out face area including beak from remaining template. Cut out the large eye circles. Produce a shape and place on previous layers.

4   Cut out branch, including feet, produce a shape in expanded polystyrene;

5   Cut out feet from template, produce shape and add to previous layers.

6   Cut out black eye centres from template, produce the two circles and place inside larger holes.

7   Cut out beak from template, produce the shape and place in position.

Diagram 11.

8   Now refer to Fig. 65. Rough breast area with a single-edged razor blade. Round edges of branch with a knife, smooth with flour-grade sandpaper and grain with a hot needle tool or soldering iron. One of these latter tools should be used to produce the radiating lines on the eyes.

Shape the beak with a knife and sand it to a smooth finish. Incise the lines on the wings with a knife.

The layers should now be glued carefully together, using the 'impact' method. The eyes may be placed so that the owl appears to look in a particular direction.

This small work, suitably painted, mounted on a painted or felt-covered oval of expanded polystyrene would make a fine piece of nursery decoration.

Cartoon figures and animals are perfect subjects for this method of working. A little light-hearted research in children's comic papers will suggest a host of possibilities.

Fig. 65. The finished work, which is 11 in. (27·9 cm.) high, prior to painting. (By the author)

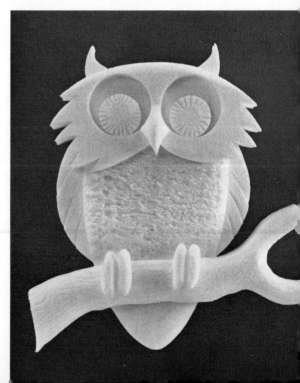

CHRISTMAS DECORATIONS

Many attractive Christmas decorations can be made in expanded polystyrene. Figs. 66–68 show simple examples of decorations produced either as simple cut-outs or by the layer method. Re-member the inflammable nature of the material and keep such pieces away from heat sources. To be safe, never place work on mantelpieces or fire surrounds where they may be knocked into the fire.

Fig. 66. (Courtesy Retail Display Service)

Fig. 68. (Courtesy Retail Display Service)

Fig. 67. (Courtesy Retail Display Service)

Fig. 69. A selection of spheres, eggs, cones and columns which are useful as basic shapes to build up Christmas and other decorations. (Courtesy S L Design Studio)

Fig. 70. A display of Christmas decorations using cones, spheres and other forms as basic shapes. (Courtesy S L Design Studio)

CARVING A MASK

Masks, of which many examples may be found in books of African culture and mythology, make excellent wall decorations. They may either be carved from 2-in. (5-cm.) material, or layered up from ceiling tiles. The mask may be curved by the method described on p. 31.

The finished carving can be painted in bright vibrant colours or grained to simulate wood (p. 26), and decorative objects such as beads, shells, small pieces of coloured glass or wood shaped to represent sharks' teeth will greatly enhance the appearance of the sculpture.

Diagram 12 (*right*). Sketches of mask forms, inspired by ancient designs.

Fig. 71 (*opposite*). This mask, 14 in. (35·6 cm.) high, has been textured to simulate wood using the scumbling method described on p. 26. (By the author)

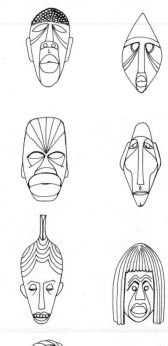

FISH SCULPTURE IN HIGH RELIEF

For beginners, the fish form is an ideal first exercise in working the material in high relief. The smooth, uncomplicated form of the fish makes it possible for even the most inexperienced to achieve first-class results. Applying the scales will afford practice in using a soldering iron or wire-texturing tools.

Sculptures up to 2 ft. (60·1 cm.) in length are effective if carved from 2-in. (5-cm.) thick material. The selected shape should be produced over a template, using one of the heat-cutting methods. Alternatively the shape may be cut with a pad-saw or fret-saw. The fins may be carved with the main body of the fish or may be applied separately after completion of the body shape.

Natural finishes are best achieved by the use of emulsion paint or acrylic paint, but a glaze may be added by applying acrylic medium or varnish.

The completed work looks well mounted on a hessian-covered panel or a textured panel of expanded polystyrene.

Stylized versions of the fish also have great possibilities. Such work may be decorated with shapes of coloured felt, thin, coloured plastic or metallic foil. Beads can also be used for scale texture.

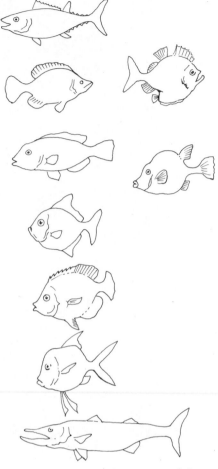

Diagram 13. Fish can take a variety of shapes and forms.

Fig. 72. Barracuda. This fish is 22 in. (55·9 cm.) long, finished in natural colouring and glazed. The background, which is also expanded polystyrene, has been worked with a hot needle to produce a reeded effect. The teeth in the open jaws of the fish presented a problem. This was overcome by producing a set of 'dentures' in expanded polystyrene. After the inside of the jaws had been painted, the 'dentures' were glued into position. Then the final delicate cutting of the teeth was carried out. (By the author)

Fig. 73. Stylized fish. Constructed from ½-in. (1 3-cm.) and 1-in. (2·5-cm.) material, covered with green and turquoise felt. Mounted on a 2-ft (60·1-cm.) panel. (By Christine Lawrence, student)

SCULPT YOUR ZODIAC SIGN

References for the signs are easily obtained from the 'horoscope' sections which appear in many magazines. It is interesting to note the many ways in which these signs are interpreted. Have a look at as many as possible, and you will then probably be sufficiently stimulated to want to produce an original design.

Material 2 in. (5 cm.) thick is ideal for work up to 2 ft. (60·1 cm.) in length. The work may of course be in ceiling-tile material and built up using the 'layering' method.

The finish is a matter of taste. The author has found that metallic paint enhances the character of the signs.

Below the Leo sign in Fig. 74, is pictured the beginnings of a Sagittarius sign, shown with the template pinned to 2-in. (5-cm.) material.

The Scorpio and Leo Zodiac signs (Fig. 75) have been carved in a bold, simple style from 2-in. (5-cm.) thick material.

In order to simplify the carving of the Twins or Gemini sign the template was cut between the two heads. The left-

Fig. 74. (By the author)

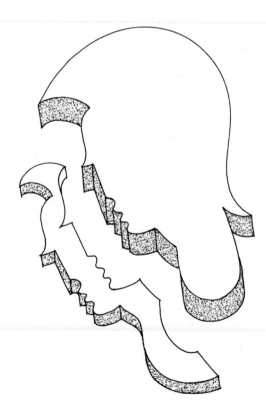

Fig. 75. A needle tool and penknife are the only
tools required to produce such work.

hand head was cut from 1-in. (2·5-cm.)
material, the head on the right from 2-in.
(5-cm.) material. After each had been
carved and textured the two pieces were
glued together (see Diagram 14). The
Twins are finished in red emulsion paint
overlaid with black. The Scorpio sign is
green emulsion paint overlaid with gold
metallic paint. The Leo sign is silver,
antiqued by an application of black
poster paint, and varnished.

Diagram 14.

58

PUPPET HEADS

Expanded polystyrene is a highly suitable material for making puppet heads. It is much quicker to use than papier mache and the lightweight nature of the material makes the puppet easier to handle than if the head were wood-carved. After painting, a final coat of acrylic medium will not only impart a glaze, but will toughen the surface considerably.

The profile should first be produced on thin card and this template used to cut the shape from the material with a hot needle or soldering iron. The features should then be roughed in with a felt-tipped pen. Carving can then commence.

Heads for hand puppets simply need a hole in them, large enough to accept a finger, cut with a knife, hot needle or soldering iron. In the case of full-sized puppets, hinging the head to the body is best achieved by gluing a stick of dowel into the neck and drilling this stick to provide the necessary hinge.

Paper clips are ideal for attaching puppet strings. Strain open the double end of the clip and apply PVA glue to this opened end. Then make a deep cut in the head of the puppet where the string is to be attached. Hold together the opened glued end and push this

Fig. 76. These puppet heads, 4 in. (10·2 cm.) high, are painted with emulsion paint. (By the author)

into the cut made. Leave exposed just enough of the clip to allow easy threading of the string. When inside the head, the opened end of the clip will tend to spring apart, pushing on the material. When the glue is dry the string will be stuck fast. This hook method is also useful for suspending panels or mobiles.

INCISED LETTERING

All students of lettering will be aware of the inscription on the Trajan column, generally accepted as being the finest example of incised lettering known. Expanded polystyrene gives the student the opportunity to incise lettering in the manner of the Romans, but without the necessity of bringing to bear the considerable skill required in working stone or marble.

Fig. 77. This lettering is 2 in. (5 cm.) high and is incised on a 2-in. (5-cm.) piece of expanded polystyrene.

The first step is to produce the lettering required on tracing or thin grease-proof paper, which should then be lightly glued to the material upon which the letter is to be incised. Glue only the outer edges of the tracing paper, and a spot in the counters of the letters, that is the holes in letters such as RBPDO etc., otherwise when the outer line of an O, for instance, is cut, the centre of the tracing will fall away. The lettering is then cut through the paper and into the material. After the incising work is completed the paper will pull away from the material easily. Any adhesive left on the incised surface may be rubbed off with the finger.

When cutting, the knife must be held at an angle. It is important that this angle remains constant, otherwise the deep centre line of the 'V'-shaped cuts will not lie in the centre of the letter forms. All cuts should, of course, be made inwards from the outside of the letter form. When producing Roman lettering the cuts must be made in long, sweeping strokes of the knife from the serifs down the stems of the letters and off on to the lower serifs. It is the need to work in this fashion that helps to develop the flow from serif to stem—so essential to the production of good Roman lettering. Incising house names is an excellent way to put this interesting exercise to practical use.

It will be found that light and shade playing on the lettering will impart a beauty to the letters not apparent in two-dimensional work, no matter how well it is executed.

CARVING A HORSE

Carving four-legged beasts of up to 12 in. (30·1 cm.) in height is greatly simplified by constructing the basic shape from two separate pieces of 2-in. (5-cm.) thick material. One piece provides the near-side body, head and legs; the other forms the off-side body, head and legs.

First, draw the horse on thin card to provide a template. From the card template first cut away the off-side legs (keeping these for use later) and produce a shape in the material.

Now take the template, fix back the cut-away, off-side legs with a scrap of gummed paper and cut away the near-side legs from the template. Produce this second shape.

These two shapes may now be joined together. Glue only the body, neck and head areas. Keep the adhesive well away from the outside edges of the shapes, as the adhesive is difficult to cut and impossible to sand when it has dried.

Now start to carve. Mark the work with a felt-tipped pen, indicating the first basic cuts and the areas to be cut away from the front and rear views. Progress carefully, checking the carving from all angles after every few cuts.

To add character, the head may be turned slightly by cutting through the neck and re-fixing it in the desired position. This should be done before carving is commenced.

Fig. 78. The card template and the near- and off-side halves of the horse cut in 2-in. (5-cm.) material.

Fig. 79. The two pieces glued together and ready for carving.

Fig. 80. This horse was inspired by an early Chinese work and produced by the above method. The decoration is applied string. The saddle cloth is a small piece of expanded polystyrene of the type sold in rolls for wall insulation. The horse is 8½ in. (21·6 cm.) high. It was painted with white acrylic paint to which acrylic medium had been added. (By the author)

20 *Picture gallery*

This section is devoted to examples of students' and artists' work in expanded polystyrene, which illustrates most of the methods and techniques described in this book. There are two parts: the first deals with low and high relief work;

the second with work 'in the round'.

The youngest contributor is nine years old. The sizes of the work shown vary from a few inches high to the 12-ft. (365·8-cm.) sculpture by James Butler, ARA.

Fig. 81 (*above*). Armoured horse. Bold texturing with a heated knife gives strength to this work which is 2 ft 6 in. (76·2 cm.) long. Finished in silver metallic paint. (By Ralph Howell)

Fig. 82 (*left*). Coat of arms, mounted on an exterior wall. Finished in bronze paint. Note the incised lettering. (By Sheila Hearsum and Marilyn Synes, students)

83 (*below*). Peter Curran, FRSA, applying finishing touches to a coat of arms. The high finish is achieved by applying plaster and sanding it. work is in full colour and varnished.

Fig. 84 (*below*). Phoenix. Finished in gold and mounted on a velvet-covered panel. (By Corinne Thomas, student)

Fig. 85. Student at work on Egyptian figures designed as properties for a window display.

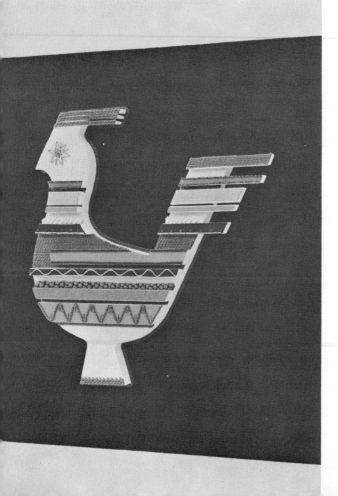

Fig. 86. Stylized bird. Layered up on a 22-in. (55·9-cm.) square panel and decorated with felts, embroidery thread and beads. (By Janet S Lipman, NDD)

Fig. 87 (*above*). Coat of arms. This work is 61 in. (40·6 cm.) high and finished in full colour. The whole was lightly coated with plaster and then sanded to achieve the smooth texture. (By Richard Colbeck, student)

Fig. 88 (*left*). Crystal. This 3-ft (91·4-cm.) high panel is composed of wedge-shaped pieces of material. Finished in greens and yellows and lightly glazed. (By Pearl Robinson)

Fig. 89. This piece of sunk relief work, 15 in. (38·1 cm.) high, shows a fragment of an ancient tablet. (By the author)

Fig. 90. A fine example of relief work. Finished in a warm oatmeal emulsion paint and discreetly antiqued by an application of a shade of this colour. Shown in position on an exterior wall. (By Stephen Saunders, student)

Fig. 91. Vegetables. This panel, 2 ft 6 in. (76·2 cm.) long, is a good example of careful layered work. (By Stephanie Grolimund, student)

Fig. 92. Reptiles. An example of high-relief work. Finished in natural colours and mounted on a hessian-covered panel, 22 in. (55·9 cm.) long. (By the author)

Fig. 93. Taurus. This work, 2 ft 6 in. (76·2 cm.) long, is boldly textured with a sculpting tool. (By Ralph Howell)

67

Fig. 94 (*left*). This work, carved in low relief from 4-in. (10·2-cm.) material, is textured with a sculpting tool, soldering iron and heated knives. (By Ralph Howell)

Fig. 95 (*below*). This fairy-tale figure, mounted on a 20-in. (50·1-cm.) high panel is carved from 2-in. (5-cm.) material. Finished with emulsion paint. (By Lesley Semple, student)

Fig. 96. This cartoon Mexican figure, 2 ft 6 in. (76·2 cm.) high, shows expanded polystyrene covered with coloured felt. The background, cactus and fence are also expanded polystyrene. (Courtesy Phyllis Hair Fashions)

(Figs. 96–104 show examples of work produced by Retail Display Service.)

Fig. 97. This wall feature, executed for a company manufacturing dry-cleaning machines, is finished with textured emulsion paint. (Courtesy Ringhoffer-Tatra (International) Ltd)

Fig. 98. These figures are finished in full colour. The male figure is 5 ft 6 in. (167·6 cm.) high. (Courtesy Ringhoffer-Tatra (International) Ltd)

Fig. 99. Work proceeding on a tyre, produced by layering material over a basic shape cut from 2-in (5-cm.) thick material. (Courtesy Trelleborg Rubber Company)

Fig. 100. The tyre after painting and varnishing.

Fig. 101.

Figs. 101 and 102 show work which is a combination of layering and carving, decorating the walls of a baby wear store. (Courtesy Baby Gear, Bishop's Food Stores Ltd)

Fig. 102.

Fig. 103. Fruit and vegetables. A display constructed of $\frac{1}{2}$-in. (1·3-cm.), 1-in. (2·5-cm.) and 2-in. (5-cm.) material. (Courtesy Budgen & Co.)

Fig. 104. Wines and spirits. This wall feature was produced in the same way as the preceding display. (Courtesy Budgen & Co.)

Fig. 105. Abstract arrangement. This work, 3 ft (91·4 cm.) high, is finished with black emulsion paint. (By Pearl Robinson)

Fig. 106 (*above*). Shell and Starfish. An excellent example of the contrasting textures which may be achieved. The irregular ground shape was textured by scraping with a razor blade. The shell and starfish were lightly covered with a skin of plaster, which was then sanded to a smooth finish. (By Stephen Bramall, student)

Fig. 107 (*left*). This table sculpture was produced by a nine-year old using a battery-operated cutter. The work is finished in greens and yellows, lightly glazed and mounted on an 8-in. (20·3-cm.), hessian-covered base. (By Melissa Howell)

74

Fig. 108. This small carving has an overall height of only 12 in. (30·1 cm.). The 'tooth' necklace was produced by gluing small slivers of matchstick to a loop of fine string. The 'bangles' are loops of thin card. Painted with emulsion paint. (By the author)

Fig. 109. Environment, 11 in. (27·9 cm.) high. Contrast the texture of the figure with the metallic smoothness of the 'skyscraper' shapes. Finished in silver. (By Michael Steward, student)

Fig. 110 (*left*). Griffon. This carving, 9 in. (22·9 cm.) high, is finished in metallic paint. (By Vanessa Crouch, student)

Fig. 111 (*left*). This 8-in. (20·3-cm.) carving is finished in black emulsion paint. (By the author)

Fig. 112 (*below*). This sculpture, about 5 ft (152·4 cm.) high, is finished in white emulsion paint. (By Elizabeth Humphries, student)

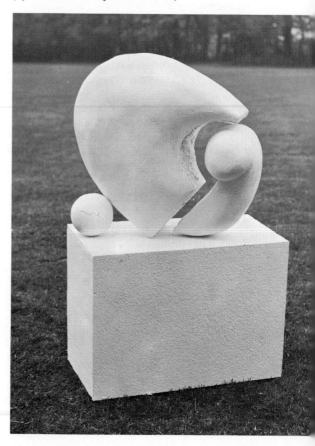

Fig. 113. Primitive. This carving, 18 in. (45·6 cm.) high, is finished to simulate wood. Note how the carving itself is treated as if the material *were* wood. (By Elizabeth Humphries)

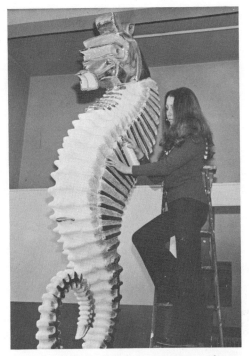

Fig. 114. Work in progress on a giant sea horse, designed for use on a carnival float. (Courtesy Clements of Watford. Display Manager R. Moppett, ABDS)

Fig. 115. Frog. The delicate legs on this work, which is only 7 in. (17·8 cm.) high, show how finely the material may be worked. The frog is supported at the back by a thin, clear, plastic rod glued into the 'rock' background. Finished in full colour and glazed. (By Stephanie Grolimund, student)

Fig. 116. Don Quixote. Carved in three pieces: the rider, the mount and the shield. These pieces were glued together and then finished in silver and antiqued with black. The lance is a knitting needle. Height 13 in. (33 cm.). (By the author)

Fig. 117. Final smoothing to one half of a 12-ft. (365·8-cm.) sea-shell. (Courtesy Clements of Watford)

Fig. 118. The segments of the dragon's body and legs are joined with string. Finished in fluorescent emulsion paint and designed to be animated under ultra-violet lighting. (By Stephanie Grolimund)

Fig. 119 (*above*). This sculpture, 2 ft. (60·1 cm.) high, is finished with textured paint. (By Elizabeth Humphries)

Fig. 120 (*left*). This work, taken from an African carving, is 6 in. (15·2 cm.) high. The decoration on the figure, horse and base is applied string. It is finished in gold and antiqued with black. (By Denise Boulton, student)

121. Julius Caesar.

Fig. 122. Roman senator.

These two sculptures are the work of James Butler, ARA, and were executed at his studio in Greenfield, Bedfordshire. They form part of a series made for the Royal Shakespeare Theatre's presentation of *Julius Caesar*.

The Roman senators are 6 ft (182·8 cm.) high. Julius Caesar himself, sculpted to the likeness of the actor playing the part, is 12 ft (365·8 cm.) in height.

The sculptures were cut from laminated blocks of expanded polystyrene measuring 6 ft × 2 ft × 2 ft (182·8 cm. × 60·1 cm. × 60·1 cm.) and 12 ft × 4 ft × 4 ft (365·8 cm. × 122 cm. × 122 cm.). A hand-saw was used to cut away the main unwanted areas. A stiff brush was used to carve the forms. Finishing was carried out with 'Surform' tools, small riflers and sandpaper.

Index

Figures in italics refer to pages on which illustrations occur